truth be bold
Serenading Life and Death in
the Age of AIDS

poems by

Julene Tripp Weaver

Finishing Line Press
Georgetown, Kentucky

truth be bold
Serenading Life and Death
in the Age of AIDS

Publisher: Leah Maines

Editor: Christen Kincaid

Front Cover Art: *The Forgotten Gods Plot Their Return to the Universe of Man.*
© 2014 By Duane Kirby Jensen, 38 3/4 x 73, Mixed media on Paper (The overall
painting is made up of 6 independent sheets 19 1/2 x 24)

Cover Design: Kayt Hoch

Author Photo: John Perkins

Printed in the USA on acid-free paper.
Order online: www.finishinglinepress.com
                   also available on amazon.com

Author inquiries and mail orders:
Finishing Line Press
P. O. Box 1626
Georgetown, Kentucky 40324
U. S. A.

Table of Contents

Dedicated to

The Babes Network
A Sisterhood of Women Facing HIV Together

What's the worst that could happen to me if I tell this truth?

—Audre Lorde

Who Would You Tell

Once a woman poet begins telling the truth, there is no end of possibilities.

—Judy Grahn

Life's truest truth, it's that truth itself unravels in ways that reveal less
not more sense or comfort.

—Tory Dent

The Addition of Audience: A Meditation

this is my coming out poem
you may think you know what that means
but I am coming out by adding you to a sacred circle
so please, bow your head
let it drop slowly—
allow your neck to stretch
feel the small cracklings,
feel whatever there is to feel

now that you feel yourself
stay inside for a minute
this is my invitation
this is my addition of you into my life,
feel how you react to what I have to tell you.

you might think you know what it is

slowly raise your head
still feeling your neck
let us look at each other

what I have to say is not easy
but I must get it out
it has been locked inside a long time
all I want from you is to witness
while staying with your own feelings
and please, for the moments after
keep your reactions silent within you
let them bounce

this is a serious coming out poem
and I am gradually preparing you;
since you barely know me it may not matter
I don't want you to distance yourself from me
remember we perhaps have more in common than different
I live, eat, work, pay bills,
enjoy going out with friends—brace yourself

I am one of you
and I have AIDS.
let's sit together with you knowing this
sit fully with yourself
seeing me, as I could be you, living with AIDS
what does it feel like?

I feel vulnerable,
but I have come to feel it is necessary
to be honest
not that I haven't been honest
but I've had a veil on
for safety, and this
right now, does not feel safe

Where are you as I add you into my life?
When was your last HIV test?
Do you think you need one?
No? Well neither did I,
the time between the test and the result was easy
because I didn't believe I would be positive

then I got the news
what fell into place
is that this truly is a lifetime about death
about remembering the names of the dead
about my loss of soul and a death wish
since the day my father died;
it is a spiritual journey.

knowledge does not make
us change our behavior
does not change our sexual fantasies

living with HIV/AIDS
I grieve the loss of full indulgence

I will always be a ball of contradictions
touching many points that do not exist.

Please slow down,
feel my news in your skin
how it affects you
I invite you to breathe
take time to feel the sensations
sit silent with me.

Unexpected

STD Clinic, Anywhere, USA
young, filled with heart, wearing a white lab coat,
regretful voice,
          Your test came back positive.

Serum-truth floods veins—
tainted—an old feeling, a sharp knife
rams hard into the pretty picture life,
fogged with clear truth.

Bubbles deflate after their thin
          translucent temporary beauty.

An average of two, maybe three years—
an expert says, a pawn for science
rooted in math and graphs.

To believe, a cure is possible
AIDS can be nullified,
Fran Peavey went from positive
to negative with no idea why or how,

her virus disappeared—I believe—
for how can one live without hope?

Fighting on such strange soil. To live beyond
the time science decreed, this war in my body
knows life during death. Inside desire lies,
          the truth of blood—
longing to live a full life, to die a natural death.

A.I.D.S.

After Lucille Clifton

it's not even a word
common   big   the side of a
bus billboard

it comes fast
this acronym   A.I.D.S.
mainlines

upstream salmon
against all odds
breath exits   razor sharp

white coat stethoscope
catches shamed face in its shine
dead gray fish sheen

this   no   word
death sentence
whirlpool drains

in the wrong direction
crosses into southern hemisphere
lynched   gouged eyes

future of empty pockets
a pocked   bloody   body
that will not   make it home

Sexual Revolution

In the mirror
it is the body she remembers
sexy as S. I. N.
it is the fucking she remembers
full fledged
hot and bothered
screaming orgasms
S. I. N.
that will never
come again

In the mirror
the body is constrained
now   scared
there is no more
free love   no more
S. I. N.
free as the '60s
love revolution and
this is s.a.d.
that reflects back
in her mirror

This body of love
that remembers
twisting hips
Amazon breasts
easy as S. I. N.
into stray palms

The price paid
twofold in this new
world after the free
reign fledged orgasms
we remember   changed
world   condoms
AIDS   all a sign of
the future that came

Sex Pays

I.
Not some mean son
out of a wood shack
carrying his axe to slash
me down—some cunt
bitch, full of, *you think*
you can write, or some
roller blade dare devil
knocking me out midway
round the track
for fun. Not these
blow-for-blow hard
muscle-AP-bullies,
billy clubs in their hands
sneer-faces distorted
mirror fun house
cadavers, tired, years
away from their art
with poisonous snake
tongues. No, give me
someone kind, orange
juice in their hand, a
pink terry cloth robe,
sugar coated words
without harm. Let me
feel such love, true
inspiration bred from
kindness, a kindred soul.

II.
What is true revelation in the story? Is it sex
pays or is it earning that first wad of cash?
It is sex pays. That a girl has a body to fall
back on, like the gay boy street hustler
kicked out of his home. Sex, a way to
earn. In it you may find a minute of kindness
or be fucked-over so bad your body is found

7

in a garbage can in an alley, a discarded
torso from one bad trick. Sex pays is
the point, some win, others lose.

Smeared Palette

She was my female craze
love at first sight
she came to interview
I want her hired.
artist, colors her talent
WAM she signs her canvas
lives life wholesale
takes neutral sweaters
cleans her brushes in broad strokes
makes art-wear I slip into
want to wear that girl
so street slick
hangs out hip hop
creates her own clothing line
she gets creative under sheets
WAMs some stray man
but when you coming home girl

out in the wild
meets six foot three, dark sculpture face
he insists she listen to his tall-talk
right on the street.
he: proud horse portrait
stops her like she stops me
his art colors onto her paint palette
crams her canvas full

he shows up at office parties
off-on again
till she meets another stray
short Latino man
sings lyrics in a band
swears its love
she spins red across her
canvas, her sheets bleed

tall dark horse stallion

is jealous, meets Julio
checks him out
exits tall, holds no claims,
he lives with another woman

strange force paints us alone
horse stallion sheds tears
misses WAM
we paint a four hour foreplay
hot wire telephone
insatiable stretch—me on an island
he travels the dark tunnel
Queens to Manhattan
knocks at my door
no condoms in any pocket
hand-to-hand we sit
big black hand traces my life line
explains how he tests negative
every six months

had I taken a cold shower
called a sponsor
been out hip hopping with WAM
or had my steady at home
but no, he came
ebony horse portrait
smooth talker
WAM hang over
free artist life
stray man on her canvas
no family connection
no high school prom
no mom no dad
just a stray
who insists his way
history paints me to her
her to him, him to me

Sex with HIV

My friend, a lesbian, tells me twice that sex with
HIV is simpler with a woman than with a man.
She knows I'm bisexual, dating the other side,
she does not know I am HIV positive.

Her theory makes no sense, with a woman I want my
tongue inside—the juices from her pussy permeating
my nostrils—I do not want a latex barrier.
A woman's musk: a perfume, a calling.

With a man, sex is containable in a little hat:
the rubber on the cock, the juices tucked away,
the insertion covered, the withdrawal intact.
Far simpler than the complexity of a woman.

When a woman orgasms she is an open cry, an orifice
begging, she can not get enough. Woman to woman
wet. And the sweet dark blood, impossible to contain,
rhythmic pulses, uterine contractions.

Lust encoded with desire for that sniff at the edge
of the panties, the ache to get inside, blood time, a natural
time of heat—orgasm the ultimate contraction—waves
of release, so how, I wonder, can sex with a woman

be simpler? With HIV, delectable fluids
must be contained—blood time laden with
danger, the smells rich and fecund, the passion
ripe, mature, like a fine wine. I've not had sex

with a woman since positive, but I imagine
oral pleasure ends, this is never talked about over
dinner, it is more taboo than sex education.

I do not ask why she thinks sex with a woman
would be simpler. I do not ask about her sex life.

Twisted Gut Desire

The goal would be to not say the word panic.
The desire would be to have you piled into me
a six-car wreck stacked metal to metal
burnt rubber tailgate hell of lust
your twisted arms cranked into my back, evil
your cigarette burnt to a nub the ashtray scattered
in my hair, dusty skull that bleeds triumphant—
piccolos I wanted to play this game so long ago.

The goal would be not to say the word panic.
The desire would be to travel across borders
guns pointed at my face—the prison door
slammed clank, clank. I have a gun hidden
in my vagina. I pull it out during climax
aim through bars and kill the only man with a key.
The opposite of love this metal I held so long
wet with juices of pomegranate.

Snake In Paradise

Canal of fire
hormonal fire
fueled by the gift
guilt gift
some snake of the Gods
slither into sex

His body next to her in the bed hot
his hard-on right there one inch from her ass
pushing, a snake between rocks
NO, she says, every cell in want
NO
Lilith knows this is not good
she has said yes too often
says yes easy

He knows her number is high
no one knows how high
him and his ex-wife
her former best friend
who used her exploits to tease

Snake enter me

Strange snake man wants to enter
wants a no-thought easy yes
hard NO she says
no snake no
deflate snake
NO

She knows his secrets
ex-wife secrets
how he used to
go to prostitutes
Puerto Rican prostitutes
black prostitutes

anything-exotic prostitutes
snake into any woman

You will not snake me
you snake my best friend
Eve from Paradise

Exotic Eve

She loves Eve
won't tell Eve
scorn
secret snake
Eve trusts her
No, she says
lying in snake breath

I do not want you
I want everyone

Man snake writhing in her butt
NO
Snake slithers into Eve
he will fuck anyone
thinks he can slide in anywhere
NO
Have to start somewhere
snake where
Start where no woman wants to go

Eve didn't say no
currency of a snake
between her legs
exchange for love
love
love and acceptance
love

she wants so bad
Eve let the snake come

Hormonal canal of fire
I say no to this guilt gift
snake of the gods

Eve can change the rug in the living room
if she doesn't like it.
Eve too can say goodbye to the snake.

Fatal Affair

I'll never meet another like him,
exotic wordsmith so slick
direct line drip into hungry pores.
Dried out, easy to catch fire, lose
control when so thirsty, and a constant
crave for distraction, easy to justify
his ravenous demeanor.

We sat on rocks in Central Park
he drew my portrait, named me beautiful
with his vision, fleeting minutes to see myself
through adoring eyes. A brief affair
will do no harm, I admire his art
where all is possible, blinded when
he paints me through his eyes, a bright
way to see a new future, my own art.

Such a beautiful spring day—
I've read James Baldwin with strong
black men who tug at my heart.
Have a dream to overcome odds,
not yet a writer, no true vision,
floating through days, falling into jobs,
relationships, no plan, not yet the
artist I long to be, I latch onto this
chance-in-a-lifetime, he enters
sucks my bones, penetrates my DNA
sinks into my spinal cord
a bad needle that hurts the rest
of my life. A shock to the girl who
drifted back-road highways.

He spent time in prison, didn't say
for what, not as vital as the urgency—
what came next—he did not want
to use a condom, said no reason or
maybe he would have, but we didn't look

very hard for the protection he assured.
Eyeing each other we moved as if we
could not live another minute without,
he swore he tested negative.

Eight years behind bars,
he asked for my trust, brain washed
in love hormones, it was only later,
the shock when I tested positive
recognized my addiction
the empty hole he filled,
brief, like a death wish.

Seeking

I have joined this story,
this family, this band
played on, this whole
household of words
to track: viral load,
T cells, triglycerides.

Numbers that rise and
fall, power to banish me
to a dark cave, into fire, or
to a royal blue no-tomorrow.
I entered this story with
knowledge, still it came

a surprise, caught in
a bear trap, speeding. A
ketchup stain transfixed
like blood on a soiled Communion
dress I wore only once. Is there
a rehearsal studio to learn

to survive? Shakespearian
CliffsNotes? The White Plague
took Keats at 25, such a romantic
story. There is so much to learn,
then ignore and carry on
like in any life.

No Answers

One learns to live with, to carry silent, to hold
without public display. The skin crawls, a
reminder that no matter the less than 20 viral

load or the stable T cells, this virus owns you.
A counter full of creams tried, tinctures applied,
a partner willing to rub applications onto my back.

Necessary touch, lucky to have such helpful
love. Especially with a slowed down sex drive,
vaginal walls drying in an aging body, post

menopause. The gynecologist has no answers,
she suggests the least cancer-causing estrogen
and a healthy lube, Luvena, with natural enzymes.

But they are helpless. She gave a good try,
despite the lack of answers. No fault,
except this so smart virus.

How We Survive

Caring for myself is not self-indulgence, it is self-preservation, and that is an act of political warfare.
—*Audre Lorde*

Blatant yet hidden, contradiction in our stride
we carry on the work we must to do to survive—

passing my friend in the hallway at work,
I had a sudden mirror hit that he was positive, too.

It made sense, why he stayed so long
and worked so hard at Lifelong, like I.

Each of us maintained a secret, aware
of the simple wisdom to exert such control.

When I told him my status, a new level of friendship.
He made a joke, called what I had *pozdar.*

Neither of us have children to carry on our legacy,
we talked of the relief to let go, allow

this life to be the end. No one ever knows
the whole of another's existence.

He's gone now, always said only what he chose to say
natural when words came to the surface

we understood self-preservation,
understood our duty to survive.

That First Lingering Opportunistic Infection

Most would love a trip, exotic travel agent who believes everything
is under control, but there is so much to do, so much to manage:

got a ticket, a packed bag, your meds, a list from your doctor,
a passport, most countries will let you in. But what happens

if you are out of town when that first infection strikes and you
don't know what's happening, everything progresses fast

let's say, shingles, covering half your head, a ball of fire
till you can't see out of one eye. Finally home, your doctor

gives a prescription, an eye patch, careful instructions.
Eventually the raging ends, but the damaged nerves never stop.

Neuralgia a constant reminder you waited too long. Maybe,
I should not have felt so brave to make my body an experiment

nor let my T cells drop below 50—it becomes harder
over time to want to travel, with so much discomfort, not

wanting to be seen with scratchy red eyes, a forehead that tingles
with pain even in the slightest breeze. It is brave just to go out

of the house. We live a long time managing skin disruptions,
the largest organ on the body, our first defense, we never

recover from damage to the nerves, the daily inflammation
to scratch, hide and cover best I can, my consequence,

despite how I tried to avoid side effects. Long ago a friend
with the same ongoing skin infections, neuralgia and dermatitis,

asked how I lived with it. I explained about skin's large surface area
suggested he focus on the places that are not itchy, said

it is not proportional, but for him, it was too much—he took his life
I'm still here, itchy, pushing forward.

There is a Drought Inside

I.

There is a drought inside
the fire of inflammation burns
cells to oblivion, the overbearing
stretch, time, its slow take-down

amplifies multiple orgasms.
Shocked at ignorance,
the body unsettled wrapped
in its fires. I waited too long,

I walk forward each step a fault
line, a field filled with dredged
up sorrow, losses incurred, but
no cane necessary. There is no rest,

no stop, for that would mean
being run over. Such magnitude to
stay alive, to thrive, take the
cocktail, but it is not enough, there is

an ongoing extinction in progress, we are
disposable. No one wants tainted blood.
Orgasm, a salve to cross this vast desert.

II.

A drought inside
secretive, disheveled
ready to strip the career once
believed in when she was another person.

Say what? How can anyone be sure
what flower will grow out of
the pointed green, this is not a rose
garden. Do not buy the farmhouse in

the country, or go for a PhD, a Masters
is adequate. He took the cake out into
the rain, the songwriter makes a metaphor
from a literal event, it turns disco

and the world changes. It was too late,
the tea dance was in its final heyday
at the last stand Fire Island. We came
home sober, vomiting from a weakened

immune system, wondering when and if
we would ever have fun again.

Eventually everyone takes the meds.

III.

There is a drought in my body
the well runs dry with no replenish,
no life plan, denial steep like
a cross to bear, how one fuck-up

happens and changes everything—
hormones change and I dry till my skin
starts cracking, my acupuncturist
points it out on the tongue, says it happens

to everyone, but when a cock enters
my walls scream, dry as a torch saying there
was enough pleasure, I disagree, but
still headed to this dry place, this

inflammatory condition speeds up
the process. All plans push forward
with an urgency to discover life's secrets
beyond our mistakes. I plot

a life across my inner desert
with nourishment, pleasuring myself
to as much wetness as I can muster.

Walking for AIDS

I step into an army of marchers.
I am already fatigued, defeated
returning home from a long war.
Some can step in and out
but when one is infected there is no exit.

I step into the long journey of marchers,
we grieve our losses in full regalia.
We each carry lists of our dead.
We are expendable.
My fellow marchers keep getting younger.
There are many more blacks, Hispanics,
and women than ever before.

Some refuse to join this army,
but they have been drafted into it.
They stand on the periphery denying
they belong here.
We marchers are the lucky ones,
fighting and walking bravely into
a bleak future.

Some bring their whole dysfunctional family.
Others come alone seeking camaraderie,
support from the crowd.
We choose to believe one another,
pair up to tell our stories.

We move forward
trying to find a cure, create a vaccine,
find alternatives and Western medicines
to add to our arsenal.

There are scientists, doctors,
lawyers and researchers who
walk long and tired.
There are social workers, therapists,

psychiatrists, and chemical dependency
professionals rising out of their addictions,
carrying others.

There are even politicians making laws
for us and against us.
There are whole armies of bystanders,
some cheer us on, others picket
or carry bombs.

Among us there are dissenters.
Those who will not protect themselves,
self-destructive suicide bombers
who have no moral sense of right and
don't care—sociopaths, anti-socials,
who see no future in the human race.

There are dancers too, healers
and visionaries, massage therapists,
poets and writers of all kinds.
Many of us have written miles of work
and have miles to go.

This is a well-beaten path with
a bushwhacking future.
It is near impossible to see anything but
a stereotypical bleak ending.
The mapmakers among us have the most
unseemly job, their charting overthrown or
ignored, laughed at, or disdained, still
we continue every effort
to map a new ending.

Come walk with us.

How Have You Helped

My dirty secret has always been that it's of course about me.

—*Eileen Myles*

I am learning to live beyond fear by living through it, and in the process learning to turn fury at my own limitations into some more creative energy.

—*Audre Lorde*

Nightmare Neutrality

A Jimmy Dean look alike,
rough white trash, he knocks her around
and she keeps going back,
must fuck her in the ass night after night.

He tells me she is a real woman.
It's rare I see her alone.
When I do, I make the most of it
        try to go beneath the surface
        ask the difficult questions about safer sex
        they do not choose to have.

They do not care about the risk,
don't talk about who infected whom,
only claim they do not use IV drugs.

I dream Jimmy Dean fucks me in the ass,
the night after I talk with her on the phone,
the night after he called looking for her.
I have to remain neutral,
No, I haven't seen her today.
Not a lie.
I am in the middle, he intimidates.
He is a big brute who feels bad and apologizes,
        smiles down into his chest,
        hangs his head in shame.
Says he didn't mean anything by it, really,
        doesn't know what got into him.

But he got into me
and I never did talk about my dream in consult,
or even in supervision.
How close I let him violate me
how scared I really was
trying to stay neutral

being very careful
what I write in my notes.

A Few Minutes at Work

Dedicated to Laurence Andrew Cave, December 18, 1961—March 17, 2016

The non-stop phone rings
I reach automatic
touch the black handle, grab my pen,
and the scrap paper
       I use to save the agency money
draw a line, a demarcation
separate one client from the next,
check—yes, the page is dated.

Hello, Julene speaking.

A client I like, *Hi Larry.*
My breath exhales
I mark his initials on the page
his profile flashes in my mind—
       When did I send him that paperwork?
       Did I receive it back?
       He's always anxious.
       Our mail system is slow
       has to be sorted
       It's most likely here
       It's only been a week
       with a weekend between
       I'll have it today, later
       Or tomorrow most likely.

He sighs, could have guessed.
He has had his fill of bureaucracies
I doodle on my scrap paper,
look at the calendar.

Setting up housing,
I wait for his release for the criminal report
       and a copy of his lease.
He must prove he pays more than 50%
       towards his rent,

and we need proof of his income
        dated within sixty days,
proof, again, of his AIDS disability.

My heart warms to his grouch.
He gave up on our housing
Now he needs to come back
        his legs don't work
        his step mom just died,
        his dad—who used to be his mom—
            has health problems.
I've know him eight years,
we hardly talk
but I know him, I doodle circles.

The red light blinks another incoming
call. Do I interrupt him?
I let it go to voice mail,
Larry wins, I'd rather listen to him
talk of the memorial for his step mom
        his second trip back east
        watching her decline since Christmas.
Doodling, I give him my time—
        it's my time too.

I have a backlog of notes
to enter into the computer
but Larry does not eat my time,
we've warmed to each other.

We click off
I check before the phone screen goes blank
        eight minutes.

The red light blinks
The phone rings
The message can wait

The provider at Bailey-Boushay with a report—
My least favorite client is acting out
going off contract with his pain meds
he may be terminated.
            Thanks for letting me know.
His initials
            I script the word fuck
            circle it with a heart.
What can I do? He'll lose nursing care
but I can't control him.

Listen to my new message—
Client in the hospital with MRSA.
Wants to know if I know where he is,
leaves a number.

Call him back—
he is grandiose, histrionic, will whine.
I dial the hospital.
Write his initials.
            MRSA, how did you get that?
            How long have you been in the hospital?
            No way I knew, do you think someone calls us?
            I'm so sorry. Glad they caught it in time.
One more day and his leg
            would have been amputated.
And he has to move and it's the holidays.
He's in a safe place, he's fine
for now. Give him some phone
            get back to work.

Training the New Case Manager to Use the Sex Questionnaire

It's part of the job to talk about sex
with men who have sex with men.
I train the new case manager, who just
graduated from a religious college.

It's routine to bring up STIs,
how HIV is spread, to those
who might not know, routine
to explore safer sex choices, we

screen only male clients. The warm up
questions start: Have you had sex
in the last six months? With a male?
With a female? We talk with openly

gay men with partners, husbands,
in committed marriages—
old fashioned moms and pops.
But we also talk to those at the far reaches

of the continuum—in open and horizontal
liaisons that consummate in parks
and bathhouses, no names exchanged.
We ask, do you carry condoms?

The goal is to elicit conversation.
Where do you go for sex?
Are you a top or a bottom?
Do you ask the person's name?

It's a part of the job, at the end,
the new case manager is pale,
says, I don't know how you ask
those questions. You will, I say.

You will.

We Sit Together in Tears

A fifty-five year old black gay man,
drug addict, living with HIV,
gets his first apartment after years homeless.

He can't follow the rules—
he lets people in to shoot up.

Loses his job at the Salvation Army,
who do not pay unemployment benefits.

Stuck with his VA pension of $700
a rent of $650, he falls behind,
worn down as his frayed baseball cap,
his tattered black leather jacket.

He needs to eat with his AIDS meds
or he has uncontrollable diarrhea—
food banks don't hand out the food he needs.

This aging veteran who served our country
cannot find work, cannot get warm.

3 a.m. comes a knock on his door.
groggy, five men push him inside
                    rape him at gunpoint.

> *They treated me like a garbage bag.*
> *If I tell anyone, they said they'll come back and kill me.*

PTSD shaken he can't believe this happened to him,
scared he'll run into them on the street.

He won't go to the police,
            what can they do for me?
He wants to get the hell out of town.

Another Heartbreak Day at Work

I work up my mojo
   but your criminal history blocks the angels.

Your stint in prison—
   your on and off use of crystal
   (with an occasional hit of heroin)
   leaves you out-of-favor to landlords,
     even those created to house
     the difficult-to-house.

You stand strong amid rejections.
I sit at home in front of a fireplace.
You live in your tent under a bridge
   move when raided, say, *I'm fine.*

We try again—
   I represent you—
Pray this time
there be leniency—forgiveness,
   a crack in the hearts
   of those who sit on a Committee
     make the final decision.

A drug habit you take or leave
treatment tried
nothing fazes you
but you age rapidly
with a bad knee—degenerative arthritis,
   not to mention AIDS
and too young for a knee replacement.

Street smart—
when cash runs out
you know which bus to take
to which mission for a hot meal.
It would be so much easier
with a warm bed, a place to cook.

The Housing Authority sees the conviction
        the warrant from Drug Court.
I see a man limping
        true to his friends.
I hear your sad story:
        split family: Puerto Rican father,
        Chinese mother, you given away
        to an orphanage
        both parents dead.

I ask you to call on
        whoever, whatever it is   you believe in.
But you expect the worst.

Your hardened eyes
        reflect the cold edge of rejection.

Sunshine

I come to work early
surprised to find you standing
waiting by the locked door
                    full of needs.
Homeless again, fired from a job
no money, looking ragged
needing meds
                    and special tests.

You ask, *Is your family well?*
In your southern politeness
            you notice my necklace,
                    compliment it.

You ask, *Is there housing?*
            A month of hotel vouchers
            if you have a plan, and
            if there is still money in the budget.

It is a small token
to help you get back on track
            off the street.
Something temporary, so you can
            have a CAT scan,
            a temporary address,
            a phone number,
            a way to be reached.

You have big plans to find a forty thousand dollar a year position.
            I've watched you lose one job after another.
HIV-positive, you don't qualify for AIDS disabled services
            there is little I can do.

I tried to reach you last week, but your email bounced.
            You give me your new email address—
                    it starts with sunshine@

I am glad you still have sunshine inside you.
You stand in the rainy snow, cold,
waiting for your case manager
        without an appointment,
                without anything but your southern hospitality
                        and a prayer for sunshine.

Glints of Crystal

Crystal is fueling most of the unsafe, binge-style sex and multiple HIV exposures.
—*Peter Staley, former ACT UP leader and founder of www.AIDSmeds.com*

Wire-thin he sits in a house
lined wall-to-wall with
foil gum wrappers.

Outside, he speed walks
avoids cracks in the sidewalk his eyes down
he watches for glints that shine—

white vans plague his mind.
His walls plastered with his collection—
slivers of silver cover floor-to-ceiling.

He lies in his bed for hours shades drawn
one light on. He stares at the glints,
they speak his language.

Sit as Sand

Glazed eyes look up at me, ask through tears,
            When can I go home?
Home to die, the words he cannot speak.
He lies in a hospital bed amassed in tubes
surrounded by machines: IV nutrition
through a vein, tubes in his nose—
mechanics maintain his body functions.
I sit still, hold his hand
ask him to blink if he hears me.
He blinks. I whisper to the angels,
            Keep him alive.

Sandy beach, I walk along
            dream him alive,
sand holds the eyes of angels.

You are seen, I murmur,
you are seen by a million sand eyes
that leak into every crack and corner.
Sand eyes open to your soul
            catch the rays of the sun
            the waves of the ocean
            the foot of the running dog.

Sand eyes call forth the gods to see you
            to survive you.
Call the desert, the beach, the ocean floor into you
let it rub your skin, give you the life impacted upon it.

A man so close to death.
I sit still, hold his hand,
            allow the pain
            become the many eyes of sand
            sending love.
                        There is nothing to say.

Sit in love, uncomfortable as it is.

Sit as sand on a beach
        sand at the bottom of a sea
        waiting for the pull of the moon.

In the Rain

Hard rainfall could wear him down.

He stumbles into the bookstore
holds up his pants with one hand
his briefcase clutched in the other.
I offer a belt he can't seem to loop.
He snaps his irritation across the room
at my attempt to help.

It took him longer than usual
to travel downtown, express bus
slow in the hard rain
slammed him down
pushed him around.
Somewhere secret he feels

weakness he will not allow.
He says, *I'm fine*
but I watch rain toss him
force his pants down.
In my face, he snaps sharp replies
confusion in his eyes.

Things are not the way
they used to be.
Before his decline,
rain was never quite so hard.
He travels rainstorms alone.
Stands up to defeat alone.

I know hard rainfall will wear him down.

Prevention for the Provider

Words come from the front desk, where a man rants at whoever will
    listen— *What are we doing about sex in the gay bars?*

Manic high-speed motor-voice grates my insides—
    AIDS cases are escalating among gay men!

His words pepper-spray-fire—mace
    AIDS workers should be doing more, things are out of control!

There are harm reduction pamphlets in our office that enrage him—
    *They encourage drug use! What are you people doing to stop the
    spread of AIDS?*

It is almost five, I instruct my hand to stop—
    do not answer the ringing phone, my ears shell-shocked from his
    shrill voice.

Afraid he will wait by the door I exit the back way, exhausted and vigilant.
    Safe on the bus I read my novel, finally the weekend, my unlisted
    phone.

I shred horseradish, prep jalapeños and onions, make a wicked chili—
    strong medicine to purge my week.

Lil' Tee

did time—
didn't say for what.

His head a shrunken dark blot
riding on top of a big white jacket.

He answers questions proper with his
New Orleans, *Yes, Ma'am*, southern speak,

he means respect to a social service
lady holding a key to survival.

Ground-up in a Texas jail, living with AIDS,
he moved north after Katrina.

I got him a cot at the shelter.
He waits for housing,

stops in daily to check.
What will you do when you get your voucher?

Get an apartment, Ma'am.
Get my GED, talk to kids in schools,

tell 'em how to get cleaner than a broke-dick dog
just like me, Ma'am.

How Often Do You Change Your Sheets?

My jailbird heroin addict client
tells me about sheets.
He only steals from big stores—chains—because
he doesn't want to hurt anyone—
big stores have insurance after all
they are protected against such things.

He tells me he changes his sheets every day.
I almost laugh, I mean really,
who changes their sheets every day?

But he insists—there is nothing
like getting into bed between clean sheets.
I wonder what it's like for him in jail
or the nights—homeless—at the local church
sleeping sheetless in the well of the stairway.

How Long Will I Live?

I'm finally making enough to pay
my bills, he said, relief in his voice,

and he repeated it, after he asked,
How long will I live? And I answered,

You can live a long time, but no one
knows for sure, each person is different.

His apartment was up against a cliff
near a ramp to a highway, no paradise,

but he and his partner were hopeful. It was
back when we were ignorant about lifespan.

I've no memory what his T cell count was
or his viral load, but I wanted him to survive,

he died soon after. Still, when I drive past his
dismal apartment building, I remember

his joy, being able to pay his bills.

This Is Not My Beautiful Life

she lives in dreams of the late '60s, early '70s
days of free love, good times
a haze of incense and marijuana
beaded curtains separate rooms
everyone walks barefoot on the earth
women wear long flowing
Indian print skirts
that gather earth energy into their wombs
they sway and dance around fires at night
their arms entwined with men in thin gauze shirts
all have long hair
there are candles, currents of romance
they live with pets that sleep on the same futon
in a lover's paradise

this is no paradise
the '60s and '70s have crashed
her starstruck lover is greasy,
unemployed, abusive
they fight about everything
their dog breeds litter after litter
of new mutts who run the house wild
she walks barefoot
steps in dog shit in their decrepit house
moldy stacks of clothing rot in piles
where dogs pee,
entwined lovemaking couples
is a faded collage
beads hang on threadbare strings
the van they lived in, traveled
across country from Rainbow Gathering
to Rainbow Gathering, sits on blocks
rusty in the back yard
there is an eviction notice on her door

she is hooked on something stronger than
marijuana these days

fresh track marks along her arm
the cornerstone of a world
not beautiful anymore

Ostrich, Please

The dream was vague, undecipherable,
let some other dream go through the rigors
of analysis, she dwells in shame, contemplates
how humankind perpetuates her situation.

She asks for chocolate sin cake
with raspberry syrup, what she really wants
is ostrich cooked well from El Gaucho.
She'll show them she has impeccable taste,

but such specialty items never show, and she
can't walk or afford to get her own.

Drying Out

I learn to settle into myself
away from my clients
such a task, to claim my time
to unroll from their problems
                    to separate

Now when the moon is full
and they are enlivened in their   pain
            the weight enters me
            a large heavy drip
            that pushes the atmosphere
            into a moisture density
            burdened with the moons
            fullness—damp weight
            that has a blues song wailing in it
                        wailing in it
            pushes tears into my eyes
                    life is unbearable
                        there is no escape

I wait for the moon to cycle
            to a lighter sentence
            to free my soul
            to sing my own song
                    in my own darkness
                    not their bleakness
I push hard
            against
                    the pain

My small earthling nervous system
cannot handle the desperate
souls of over fifty grown adults
who tell their stories
their histories bereft—

to listen

saddens *any* recipient

Too much dampness
    in Chinese medicine
        slows one down
            makes the system slow
                to heal

Too much dampness
    is a classic Western affliction
        and you bring it all to me
            in tears, in anger
            in psychotic breaks
            in abusive relationships

Stories you pass on careless,
furthering their impact casually
        as if the telling might help

But I stop you mid-sentence
I do not need to hear it all
in fact I encourage you to let go
        find new resources

The danger in dampness—
        it may never dry out
        it will lead to rot

How We Fail

> Not I—Not anyone else, can travel that road for you, you must travel it
> for yourself.
> —*Walt Whitman*

We cannot transport you in our car.

We cannot hold your hand through life.

We cannot come identify you when you are inducted
      and need your identity confirmed.
We will call 911,
ask for a wellness check.

We cannot post your bail or accept collect calls from jail.

We cannot.

The expectation is that you live your life
      without us standing directly by your side.

We cannot take your mail out of your mailbox
open it for you, fill out your forms.

We cannot come and prevent you from setting your house on fire,
      pick up the butts you drop on the floor.

We might be able to put chore services in place,

Maybe.

We cannot pick you up at the hospital door
after your minor surgery.

We may want to do these things at times.
We want to make sure you get on the bus
      that takes you to treatment
      we've made ten thousand calls
After we've squeezed the assessment in early

at your insistence.

But certain steps only you can take.
Certain moves only come down to one.

One person.

You.

Your life.

Your responsibility.

Your time
to take
the step
only you can make.
Get on the bus.
Open your mail.
Call a friend for a ride.
Agree you need more care.
Decide it is time
        to become clean and sober,
                go to treatment,
                        take your meds right.

Who Have You Lost

Implicit in poetry is the notion that we are deepened by heartbreaks,
that we are not so much diminished as enlarged by grief,
by our refusal to vanish—to let others vanish—without
leaving a verbal record.

—*Edward Hirsch*

One of the first steps in making the private grief public is the ritual
of memorials. I have loved the way memorials take the absence of
a human being and make them somehow physical with the use of sound.

—*David Wojnarowicz*

Vanishing Point

For Gaëtan Dugas, the so-called "patient zero" of the AIDS epidemic

Man one: catches a monkey virus
He walks, flies, travels, fornicates for years
His light shines bright.

Man two: gets sick with a rare pneumonia.

The first man: develops large purple spots
ruining his sex appeal
A star flickers
light fades into the black sky.

The second man: cannot stop coughing
no one knows what is wrong.

Isolated incidents spread
Hospitals report to public health
A lone nurse registers alarm
staring at crossed-hatched graphs.

We all vanish on her bell curve
death traveling nanocells point-to-point.

Frantic she watches young men
fall into the black hole, unable to sleep
with so many common denominators.

Man one: dies etched on her chart
A rare Mediterranean disease takes him.

Patient zero: finally at his death distance.

That nurse
saw the future
tried to warn us.

Stonewall

I still mourn Judy Garland
with the queers at Stonewall—
I was one of the flamboyant ones
who'd had enough. Salt-sweat
mascara running my face
getting on with my grief for
my girl. Cop raid ire-fire
this is my right, my life,
you bet I snapped.
Don't push us
when we mourn.

Judy Garland (June 10, 1922–June 22, 1969)

The Sarcoma Scourge

There were whispers, *Mediterranean,*
      rare   regional
                  only old men get it.

Kaposi sarcoma made marks
on gay men's skin
tagged their torsos, branded their legs
made their face a target like wearing a
pink triangle
         a damn holocaust inside our bodies

disco getting a bad rap
poppers feared

my friend freaked when she heard
a lesbian got the virus.

Conspiracy theories leaked
from party balloons after hours

night clubs dying
friends calling in a panic
each new rash or bump

end of life predictions
angels came out from closets to
ACT UP meetings, our new
Community, we had to have a say.

Keith Haring, known for his art,
died. It was 1990 with so many
losses, AZT equaled death

and our president
refused to say AIDS.
This filibuster infection activated us

to make noise, create buyers clubs.
We drank blood from organic liver
in an alley from a cooler

did anything, to save our lives.

Water Rat Boy

Dedicated to Jimi Heath, died July 15, 2003, on his thirty-fifth birthday

Lunchtime
I sit at my computer
wait for your tap—
appointment we made to buffer
       your way to court.

Wet water rat, you pull at my heart.

Two taps, soft
barely a disturbance—
I turn to see you dripping in the rain
       you clutch a damp page
          wave it at me, a letter in pencil.

Sad little boy grown man
scruffy beard, handwriting so bad.
I sit you down with pen and pad
       instruct, *write neat as you can.*
My stomach glad you made it.

I construct a letter too—
       two letters better than one
       to help water rat swim to safety,
       a new shore, dry up, learn to fly.
Invested to help you stay out of jail,

       stay clean, keep your housing.
May my assistance offer saving grace
       this work I do barely enough.
My offer to a drowning rat boy—
       lunchtime skipped.

My paycheck the only reason I know you.
When I change jobs, never see you again

I will remember you soggy wet
your frail taps
your words dripping off the page

your fear of leaving your solution
that dear stability—jail—
structure behind bars:
safety, sobriety and rules to follow.
Your eyes seeking hope.

Only What I Can Do

Dedicated to Juan Bernal, died September 9, 2001, at age 41

I write a letter for my client today.
I sit with him on the deck
of the skilled nursing facility.
He eats breakfast, smokes cigarettes.
He wants me to write to his baby brother
                              in jail doing time.
He dictates: *I love you—*
I need a thousand dollars—
I will drive the get-away car.
He has these plans
he needs to convey—tells me
his little brother will tote the gun.

He dictates: *The doctor told me today*
I am dying, but he doesn't know
how long it might take.

It is doubtful he will be able to drive
the get-away car when his legs are paralyzed
and two people have to transfer him
from his bed to his wheelchair and back.
He has a direct line morphine drip
he presses every ten minutes.

It is doubtful he will make it
home again, but he wants to go home.
He drifts in and out of sleep, nodding-out
his thoughts stop in mid-sentence,
he loses track of his message to his brother.

He asks if they'll read his letter.
The jail will, I say. He edits out the question
about whether his brother killed someone.
He thinks he did. I suggest he
take out the part about robbing a bank
but he doesn't. He thinks it's a good plan.

Kass's Organized Funeral

Dedicated to Kass Anderton, passed on February 27, 1997 at 47 years old

It was a good day to cry
in a good year to die
and a good life to celebrate.

Kass planned everything
every last detail—
the white lilies draped across her casket;
songs sung by her good friend,
a former priest.

His voice resounded,
cascading off the cathedral ceiling,
brought tears to our eyes.
We took communion
exactly as she wanted us to, at St. Joseph's.

We make a commitment in our hearts
to continue what she started,
to carry on her dream, the organization
she founded, Babes.

We wallowed in our love,
in appreciation of her efforts,
her memorial a reminder to plan our own funerals,
to stay politically active, to keep doing
whatever it is we must do for those of us
living with AIDS.

We circulated her scrapbooks
a mischievous angel peeked out from photos,
see me
the seeds I sow will long be remembered.

Her joy, the equivalent of many lifetimes
present, yet anguished, for all she might have done

had she not been disabled by Marfan syndrome
and contracted HIV. She lived well beyond
morality expectations despite her double disease.

She left her mark, supporting all living with HIV
no matter how they were infected.

Her mantra—
not much in common—
but she did not take a back seat
she embraced us at her *bring your favorite
take-out* gatherings at her home.
In her living room we started an organization
wrote the first draft proposal for Ryan White Funding
on her computer.

With her steady companion cane, and her black humor
she drafted a questionnaire to spoof
a medical intake, we all filled it out.
So much fun we devised from this disease
we laughed hearty, the best medicine.

Not much in common,
but she sat with us common folk.
Corrected those who tagged her a good AIDS patient,
put them in their place.
She wanted to do a theatre piece
put her ideas out to the world, but
she died first. Babes kept this commitment
we did not let her down.

At the hospital for months
with one goal, to go home
insistent she said, *I need to buy another house
with better access.*
Her case manager asked,

Do you really think you're up to buying a house right now?
She went home and held court 'til she died.

Rebel Rouser

Dedicated to Allyson Hunter, July 1, 1959—September 24, 1999

ACT UP Rebel Rouser
we found you, a lesbian with AIDS in Seattle
so many didn't think that was possible
yet we had two in our small group.

We remember your hair—long down your back,
fire-red, then
        shaved bald overnight
        you started chemo
        didn't want to talk about it.

We remember the illusive hope for a cure
you carried to your grave—a member of ACT UP—
how the police carted you off to jail.

We miss your endless courage.
We survivors still wait for the cure.
We feel you watching
        when AIDS funding is cut
        while infections continue.

A heart so brave,
           to die so young.
You fought each round
walked with a cane.
Women came and went from your life
        some stayed longer, till they
        couldn't take the heat.

Locked away those last years,
rare to see you, a picnic here,
        an occasional party,
        a march down Broadway.

There was no more time

You said your truth—
To say the meds are anything less than chemotherapy is ridiculous—
and stopped the meds.
   we thank you
   every living day
   your ashes on our windowsills.

—

Jim

Jim loved trains, on his birthday friends take
a special train with his urn, scatter his ashes
in his favorite mountains of Oregon.

Jim loved sour cream lemon pie, coconut cream pie
he ate at Dahlia's, drank a fine wine. When he became
too nauseated to eat, he had a plan and a secret stash.

Certain losses no one can tolerate.
Jim loved to travel south, visit fields of Iris
he bought bulbs and planted them in his garden.

Today I am blessed with yellow Iris
in full smile, on my table they gather love
from the sun, remind me of Jim.

Keep Hope Alive

Dedicated to Ed Aaron, died September 11, 2002 just after midnight, age 49

I go to see Ed
at the end of my day
the last of my priorities
before my birthday tomorrow.
A skeletal figure greets me,
I comment on how thin he is.
His voice low in his throat
his breath a rasp, labored.
I bend down over his bed, listen hard
tune out the traffic from the street.
Barely audible he says, *I had a sore throat,*
       it's better now, but I'm wasting.

                    I'm dying.
                    I have to be realistic.
It's a good idea, I agree.

Exhausted from this exchange
his eyes roll back in his head
a yellow slit is all I see.
He looks like an alien.
Don't let him die now I pray.
I watch his breath
ask if he is tired
get no response so I let him sleep
until I remember he needs to sign a form.

I rouse him
we make a joint effort to sit him up.
I raise the electrical bed, take his hands,
He strains, coughs huge globs of phlegm,
I reach for tissue
he for the bed cover.
I contain my repulsion
help him get decent.

We work hard to sit-up position
I direct his hand to the line
watch his attempt at
chicken scratch wavers.

His robe open in the back
rides up his legs
exposes the dark rings
of Kaposi sarcoma sores.
He tells me, *The chemo is winning,*
                my KS is disappearing.
That's good, I say.

His nurse comes in
checks his breathing
says he is doing good today
reminds him there will be blood tests daily.
A line hangs out of his neck
his veins too far-gone.
These next couple of days critical—
this last round of chemo
hard.

She reminds him, drink Ensure or Boost.
                I ate chicken today.
She says nutritional supplements are better, then
she asks the critical question,
"If your heart stops, do you want us to pound on your chest?"
        Yes, Hope floods into his eyes.
                Forget what I said earlier.
That you are dying? I ask.
                Yes, keep hope alive for me.

Unforgettable Memorial

Dedicated to Michael Misrok, December 20, 1962—May 1, 1997

Tonight, when I see your wife, meet
her new husband, I swallow tears hard
hold the words in my throat—
                    How is Michael?

At your funeral—busting out
you danced to hard rock, I mean bogiedown
danced for the camera,
in your best Louis Armstrong
you sang—
                    Remember me as sexy.

Stick-thin, hair tossing over shy eyes
                    34 years old
Microphone-led rockabilly tour—
you introduced your three cats, three cars—
shared the precious
                    memorabilia of your life.

Our star volunteer—I nominated you
for our award. A video producer
your creative eye made our agency proud.
The night of the ceremony
rushed to the ER—pneumonia, wasting—
                    the start of your final days.

I carried your prize to the hospital
A glass heart full of blood red swirls.

Happy in Hawaii

She lived in a smoke-laden trailer
in Woodinville destined to be razed
she walked laps on her StairMaster,
lit one cigarette after another, stopped
taking her AIDS meds, tired
of the seizures, and her doctor,
his unfulfilled promise to find an answer.

Who would ever touch her again
the way a woman wants to be touched?
She'd lived in Hawaii once, wanted
to go back, but had no way. In a photo
on her sideboard she had big hair,
a drink in her hand, happy in Hawaii.

Her mother found her dead
on her couch, alone in her trailer,
only 45, a skinny woman with flat
hair, no car, no friends.
May she find a sunlit beach,
warm water, white sand.

Special Order

His last wish was a bottle of salad dressing that cost
thirty-two dollars.
Thought I'd have to special order it,
would have taken too long.
Lucky I found one store in Seattle that carries it.

What would I want before I die?
A large strawberry milkshake would be perfect.
I'll change my mind come next week.

These new drugs may save my life
I may not need your services anymore.

Yes, keep living
go away
let this insanity end.

In the meantime, it's a good idea to
do your power of attorney,
make your will, have a living will ready, just in case.

And, you might think about
what it is you want to eat before you die,
so if it needs to be special ordered
there will be enough time.

Rick, a Lonely Death

His partner died before him.
He has no friends in his room.
No Christmas tree.
No cards or flowers.
Just a picture of himself in drag—
from a more glorious time
when he was a beautiful woman,
full faced with makeup and a wig,
draped in an evening gown,
unrecognizable but for the sparkle in his eyes.

He stares at me now, unable to answer questions.
I stop asking, sit, hold his hand.
I look from him to his picture and back.

Last time I saw him,
he talked about going home,
going back to work.
Said he hadn't realized how sick he was,
how much help he needed
with all this care.
He expected to get better.

Encephalitis eats up his brain,
drains his body into these final days.
He does not want to die.

I squeeze his hand, say, I must go now.
He smiles, says *Okay,* easy going, then,
                    I love you.
I love you too, I say.
I walk out slowly,
contain my desire to cry,
to run far away and scream.
I want to bring him back
to the life he wants so badly—
to the yesterdays of dress up and party
and care no more.

Eli

Eli got too tired to use the stairs,
            no longer helped co-workers
            move boxes of brochures.
We noticed he sat at his desk more
            didn't do home visits as often.

Eli couldn't keep his secret
but didn't have the energy to tell us.
His face blotchy
            he hid behind paperwork,
            didn't socialize during lunch.

He wanted to be part of the work force
            wanted to be useful
            after being on disability four years.
He was a social worker.
If only he had not come back,
            to this particular work
            I believe he would have lived.

One year after he re-started work he died.

We decide to plant a plum tree
            in the park in his name.
It takes a year to arrange the planting,
            for the soil to be ready.
The day we plant, it rains.

His tree overlooks Puget Sound.
Eli liked this park where
people walk their dogs, jog.
Each spring
            pink blossoms bloom Eli alive.

Aftermath

the son dies
he wanted everything to go to his partner
but he never got around to making a will
his mother called him every so often
always asked after his partner
he didn't think it would be a big deal
they built everything together
worked hard, and when he couldn't
it was his partner who was there
his partner who kept working on the house
did extra work to care for him
ran to the hospital daily
made sure he was able to return home
helped with all the arrangements for a hospital bed
so he never got to the will
it was too busy all the time
he got too tired

and the aftermath
it was a good thing he wasn't around
to witness his mother's aggression
taking the house with the patio
and the fireplace he tiled with his partner
selling it for profit
right out from under the man
who was half owner
but not officially on the mortgage
he didn't get a penny
didn't get anything
except his clothing, some photographs
and a new start he never expected

One Stirs All the Others

Dedicated to Bruce McIntosh, August 4, 1946—March 12, 2003

1.

One cannot be prepared for death
cannot hold the appointment calendar in the hand
point at that one day and say, this is it.

One death brings up all others,
the World's Fair I never went to with my father
me standing alone next to a crazy mother.

At Dad's funeral I understood
I would be alone from his death on
I wept alongside the bank of a stream

I gave up daffodils.
I missed seeing Bruce at his death
I wanted to see him one more time

to sit with him, be part of his inner
circle, to laugh together.
His death an angry opera

composed by his liver.
A long-term survivor
who *kept waiting for the ball to drop*;

his life full tilt to the end
his story—how he learned to love
the opera side-by-side with his partner—

at the pinnacle of this AIDS epidemic
he survived decades, till his liver
brought him down, he would say

he died surviving AIDS,

he would say, the AIDS community
with a scoff, he hated that phrase

claimed there was no such thing.
That day I looked at him and knew.
Simply knew, then, how open he was.

2.

Go now to what waits
let go the rain of Seattle
the loves of your life
that brief spark of time

Go now into the darkness
to find the next journey
the next incarnation

Let go the soft thunder rumble in the distance
the lightening jagged in the sky
cross over into that world we stare at in wonder
we quake in our human fears
go peaceful, take this walk, this brave leap
into the mystery

Let go the liver's complications
the fine glass of red wine
Let go the gastronomic feast
shared at Sunday brunch

> *From Bruce's last journal entry (3/5/03), "...death is no foe at all, but a dark, rather mysterious handsome stranger who offers peace and quiet and an end to struggle, stupidity, strife and pain."*

Her Last Walk

Dedicated to Kass Anderton, Babes Network founder

1.

have you seen dead men walking?
not the movie,
men in real life
thin as rails
holding canes and walkers
young men in wheel chairs
skin and bone
pale ashen gray

dead men walking with IV poles
dead men standing
then tired
one more day at a time
in pain, on pills
body riddled with this or that infection
and no T cells left to man their army
no struggle

angry at the system
victimized by the disease
at peace with their end
or in denial
they are not brave warriors
they are dead men walking
on numb feet

afraid to lose precious life
they hobble, stumble
one day to the next
they move slowly through time
they want to do so much more
energy burns rapid
infections, fever, night sweats and

weak bowels break through

2.

men is metaphorical
dead women walk too
dead women push boundaries
stand on airplanes
with their IV poles
take a stand when denied access
what do you mean I cannot get on this plane
I have a ticket, I paid good money
dead women walking
do not go down easy,
sometimes fast, never easy

3.

I walk in denial
healthy denial
I walk a long journey
before the cane, walker, wheel
chair or numbness
I walk strong
in denial
that I am going to survive
I walk a dead woman's walk
strong as I can

Ode to Homeopathic Growth Factors

*Dedicated to Barbara Brewitt, PhD, Molecular Biologist
and Biophysics October 7, 1948—August 25, 2009*

Sir Cell Signal Enhancers
infuse my body
with memories of how to stay well.
Be a bridge of low-key subtle love
into my immune killer cells.

Your kiss of health: sleuth signals
issuing gentle reminders. Oh, Sir Growth Factor,
you tip your hat, say, excuse me my dears,
I've this joyous message to bear,
and then hand-off to my cells—
        the imprint
        the code
        the command—
reminded they go back to their initial duty.

My cells come welcoming.
Weary they reach out their hands,
accept and say, thank you
we are tired, very tired.
Your imprint revives
our weak wiggling bodies
we waken brimming to the edge
like we just drank our first morning
coffee. Freshly
coded we jump back
refreshed
to do our daily work
simple, but difficult tasks
to keep a body healthy.
A reminder to each cell, do not give up,
do not die, our commands intact:
we fight off infection.

Oh, glorious Sir—homeopathic love
come knock three times each day
help us remember
how to win.

How Do You Survive

The artist, and particularly the poet, is always an anarchist
in the best sense of the word.
He must heed only the call that arises within him
from three strong voices: the voice of death,
with all its foreboding, the voice of love and the voice of art.

—*Frederick Garcia Lorca*

Silence can pose a greater threat than the difficult truth.

—*Harriet Lerner*

Old Timers, the Women

us old timers
dwindled down to three who show up
loaded with goodies
I made the salad, picked up bread
and cheese. The girls bring crackers
more cheese and shumai
they do not forget dessert—key lime pie
a berry sponge cake concoction—
we eat until we can eat no more

we catch up on each other's lives
new work, recent losses
our latest vacations,
the state of our mothers
who are slowly leaving us—
right after trips home to visit they decide to die—
and then we experience the reemergence of our periods
as if our mothers are reminding us
we are women, even with AIDS
and there is so much to speculate about—
how the meds impact our menopause

all this talk tires us
and it is time to go
lucky one can still drive the other home
there is a memorial next Saturday
at 3 p.m.—there will be a planting of bamboo,
ashes will be buried underneath—

our lives are full of ashes
some of us blend them in pavers for our patios
others have them in jars on windowsills
in urns above the fireplace

our emotions are right on the surface
bubbles ready to pop
tears and the flow of anger are storms

that ride our intestines
and spill our guts with necessity
we stand strong in the flux
from easy laughter to weeping
glad to have each other

                        still

I Would Have Said No

I started a project to prove,
beyond the realm of doubt
there is a cure for AIDS,
but it went awry.
Dissidents and Denialists
smile behind their masks.

All I wanted was to hold you,
that tall tight body angular and lean,
such a brooch, a sleek metronome,
its beat against my breast,
my corn-patterned quilt wrapped
us cushioned against cold wind.

I might break down, wear sunscreen
follow you into the ocean, lie on a beach.

I told you my father cradled me
told you how your DNA sings to mine,
like sorry water in a quaking world.
At death one knows how precious
each moment. We shared hot chocolate, but
we'll never sit in its sweet vapors again.

If I could have married you
I would have said no. I wanted freedom.

In the Evening

> *The skull on the poet's desk is the most well-known*
> memento mori, *Latin for "Remember that you must die."*
> *The Elizabethan fashion to keep a skull on the writing desk*
> *served as a reminder of the futility of human endeavors, of*
> *life's brevity and uncertainty.*

I sit and read an article—
a forty-one year old publisher
had a brain aneurysm, he lives
to write about waking up paralyzed.

I insist, read this.

Later, you find me, article half read,
tears in your eyes.
Recent executor of your father's estate
you learned things I will never cross—

there is the fact of our wills
all the steps of dying
we have yet to lay out—
mementos we would rather avoid.

We sit quiet in the darkening living room
ponder life-forced events,
the theft of our car
the war on the other side of the world.

The simple flutter of butterfly wings
how their affect on love goes unnoticed.

Another Cure for AIDS

There are ozone and filters,
and sonic waves that will kill the virus
These are cures one must believe in
to make them real.

Here's a man who is a representative
for the cure of AIDS
for all the Northwest territories
And for all of France
and this is cutting edge technology
And the crazy thing is
I want to believe him.

The cure, he tells me, is very expensive.
An air filter system
that kills microorganisms and viruses.
Hotels are buying it, two so far.
Hospitals all need it.
All airplanes should have them.

There is a huge market
because of how polluted
we have made our lives.

And it makes sense
like so many other crazy ideas
people grasp onto
seeking answers
where there are none.

Reflections on HIV

It won't roll over, play dead for its host. It is ignorant about your
foreclosure, or that favorite car you bought back when you considered
yourself employable.

It doesn't appreciate your pleasure, how you enjoy walking barefoot on
the beach.

It won't do daily tasks: organize its pillbox with prescribed
antiretrovirals, make sure you eat the right amount of fat. It adores a tall
Pina Colada that suppresses your T cells.

Certainly, it never reminds the immune system of its job, it is
preoccupied with replicating, surging by the billions through your
body, selfishly thriving.

But it is not smart enough to realize it causes its own death.

Hidden stowaways, sly viral RNA particles stored, waiting in lymph
nodes, spinal fluid, the brain, it adapts into mutant forms,

multicultural, they turn your body against itself: mitochondria die,
cheeks curve inward hollow from the inside out, toes turn numb.

Deformities accelerate. You try alternative therapies, but
it is no use against this mammoth that teaches a secret of life:

the impermanence of time. In calculations for life expectancy, it speeds
up the formula. It is the great awakener to fate,

traveling with your body to its own bitter end.

Penciling, Again, Through the Phone Book

Who do you call after midnight
when all your friends have died?

I live so alone
with my address book
full of crossed out names.

Death slows me down
                others keep rushing.

The last time I was sick
in the hospital sick,
in the nursing home sick,
getting tested for cancer,
finding out body parts
don't work anymore—

The world kept rushing
            my rent still due
                    no one left to call.

Meditation on Mortality

It will be okay—everything works out
as it is meant to. Really, is it okay?
We have a choice to view life this way.
I stare out my window at my serene street
I grow old and closer to a hoped for
peaceful death. My windowsill paint chips
on its natural progression of decay—

like the wasp who somehow flew in, flinging
herself at the window: Tap. Tap. Tap. To
escape, to live—I will not mess with her
death, will not try to save her, she will live
alongside me until she disappears, to be found
on some cleaning binge fallen in a corner,
a mere shell, light as a wisp of feather, yellow
stripes a surprise of beauty, or maybe she'll
die under a light, be the dark spot in a fixture
that only comes down when a bulb dies.

I tell this yellow jacket, *It'll be okay, your death*
will be okay, you will not get back to your hive
home, never fulfill your natural insect life
because you found an open crack, flew in,
now you are living regret. Tap. Tap. Tap.

I could help, I could get stung. Yellow jacket,
your sting sharp, I remember it as a child,
opening a window, one of your ancestors a sudden
surprise, my screams brought Grandmother running,
my arm red and swollen. She held me, gave
first aid, wiped my tears. So fast, caught off guard.

So, I will not mess with you yellow jacket and you
better not mess with me. Your life will end here,
my home a resting ground for insects caught;
their taps insistent. You wander my blue vase—
I sit and watch you chart territory, if you move

close I will exit my rocking chair. The door
to the bedroom closed, the door to the office too.
I will not tangle with your dying. Will not
express the urgency of fear. I want to
believe in comfort for you and for me.

HIV Today

We long term survivors
got a lifetime, came through the hard
years still strong. Smart not to trust early.
The only answer at the beginning, AZT,
we found our own box of hope
filled a whole book with reasons
to live, made art, wrote stories, poems,
created family.

We felt love for our dying
brothers and sisters, wanted them
to fall well, we held community
created an embrace: ACT UP meetings,
coalitions, die-ins. We made history.
Moved science up a notch
like that last lover in our belt,
that quilt panel we've all made.

Those of us still here with
our endless days to live
take pills daily to hold steady.
Victory survivors
welding a healing path
with our scrapbooks we created, *Hope*,
its title, and for some of us
our hearts melded to welcome this virus
make it feel at home. Give it a long life.

Larks

All the beautiful gay men—
piano appassionato
glamorous
        their manhood bent
        betrayed this life
        outcasts to continuance
        their bootless sobs

        larks—they sang
cruising this inner passage

On my path the weather has been
grey
        adaptive survivor
        (yet) it is you, each lark, who made life
                easier
        difficult trip into
                tolerable adventure

to touch such life
in the shadows at the gay disco
dancing with you in your glory

Destined to Be Here, Still

Reflections on the 2nd National Long Term Survivor's Day
(June 5, 2015)

My magical thinking mind acted out, a foolish brokenwing
fledgling running wild from heartache, missing
my dear departed dad. My guardian angel,

protection from harm, like an inoculation to survive.
But caught off guard with holes in my aura: smoking
pot, snorting a line, center stage in the sexual revolution

with nothing to hold this vanguard back. Freedom, a goal
to achieve like a crown. An impervious mind believes
it will incur no harm, no demon disease without a cure.

Might belief in immunity be a strength when the unforeseen
comes around? HIV the cross our generation has to bear: it
shattered our revolution and disproved the lie: all will be fine.

Destiny to stay strong. Mercury in my chart a prophecy
foretold: You will work with young sick men. On this
Long Term Survivors Day celebrating twenty-five years,

I remember my long list of the dead, hold gratitude for my dad
who died too young, for friends still here, for the man
who stayed despite my infection, and yes even for HIV.

Green Witch with AIDS

I walk with my toes afire
I am not safe within my walls
    I shoulder many dark secrets
I am not a cavity
    I am as deep as the ocean
I am not female song
    I am an ethereal being
I am not just partner to a man
    I am full unto myself
I am not a female
    I'm a planet
I am not a slut
    I'm a sacred virgin goddess whore
I am not a stupid girl
    I'm a wise witch
I am not a diamond in the rough
    I'm a rainbow over the sky
I am not a crazy loon
    I am Cassandra singing

Notes

The poem *Unexpected* refers to Fran Peavey.

Fran Peavey was HIV-positive and on AIDS medications when she wrote a book about her experience, *A Shallow Pool of Time: An HIV+ Woman Grapples with the AIDS Epidemic*. She led workshops worldwide and planned to go to India to continue her work. She had to get tested for her visa and the test came back negative. In a later book, *By Life's Grace: Musings on the Essence of Social Change*, she has a chapter on this experience. I met her at one of her workshops and asked her if she knew how her status changed. She said she had no idea. She passed away in 2010 at age 69.

The poem *Ode to Homeopathic Growth Hormones* is dedicated to Barbara Brewitt, PhD.

Her obituary in *The Seattle Times* (October 4, 2009) read,

> Through her doctoral studies and research at the University of Washington School of Medicine in Biological Structure (Ph.D '89) and a post-doctoral fellowship at the National Institutes of Health, Brewitt was recognized as an international expert on cell-to-cell communication, broadening the understanding of growth factors (cell signalers) as related to health... By combining the doctrines of molecular biology and biophysics with 250 years of natural homeopathic medicine, Brewitt created safe, clinically proven, oral homeopathic delivery of nine different cell signaling formulas that addressed symptoms associated with ailments such as HIV, Autism, PTSD, hormone and age-related imbalances. Nine national and international patents were held. The company's two most notable clinical research studies were with orphaned children infected with HIV in South Africa and studies on anti-aging using homeopathic Human Growth Hormone (hGH). Brewitt was one of the researchers helping Autistic children (ASD) in the PBS documentary "Finding the Words."

Acknowledgements

These poems originally appeared, sometimes in different versions or with different titles, in the following publications.

Gertrude and *HIV Here & Now*, "Sexual Revolution" / *Menacing Hedge*, "Sex Pays" / *Cliterature*, "Twisted Gut Desire" / *Arnazella*, "Sunshine" / *Nerve Cowboy*, "How Often Do You Change Your Sheets," "Only What I Can Do," "Happy in Hawaii" / *Las Cruces Poets & Writers Magazine & Pontoon*, "This is Not My Beautiful Life" / *Blue Collar Review*, "How We Fail" / *Qarrtsiluni*, "Stonewall" / *Babes Talking Newsletter*, "Kass's Organized Funeral" and "Rebel Rouser" / *The Healing Muse*, "Keep Hope Alive" / *Pirene's Fountain*, "In the Evening" / *Main Street Rag*, "Another Cure for AIDS" / *The Unprecedented Review*, and *HIV Here & Now* "Green Witch with AIDS"

The author acknowledges the following anthologies in which these poems appeared, sometimes in different versions or with different titles.

Ghost Town Poetry, Volume 2, "Sexual Revolution" / *Under a Silver Sky: An Anthology of Pacific Northwest Poetry*, Volume 1, Evergreen College, "Smeared Palate" / *Northwind Anthology*, 2008, "A.I.D.S.," "In the Rain," and "Special Order" / The Writer's Almanac & Garrison Keillor's *Good Poems, American Places*, "Only What I Can Do"

The poem "Her Last Walk" under the title "Death Walk" won third place in the Unfinished Works Competition, of AIDS Services Foundation of Orange County, and appeared in the competition catalogue.

"Old Timers, The Women" was used in the visual and verbal installation *Vernacular: A HIV/AIDS Documentary* produced by Joe Plotts and Dan Weiser, exhibited at Priceless Works Gallery in Seattle.

The following poems appeared in the chapbook, *Case Walking: An AIDS Case Manager Wails Her Blues*: "A.I.D.S.," "Another Heartbreak Day at Work," "Sit as Sand," "In the Rain," "Prevention for the Provider," "How Often Do You Change Your Sheets?," "Water Rat Boy," "This is Not My Beautiful Life," "How We Fail," "Only What I Can Do," "Keep Hope Alive," "Special Order," "Rick, A Lonely Life," "Aftermath," "Penciling Again, Through the Phone Book," "Death Walk," and "Another Cure for AIDS."

Thank you to Finishing Line Press for publishing this full body of my HIV/AIDS poems and to Leah Maines for selecting my manuscript. Thanks to my friend and poetry partner Kayt Hoch, who designed the cover for both my books that feature HIV poems; without her support this work would not be the finest book it could be. I am grateful to Duane Kirby Jensen for his art, which now graces my two full size poetry books. A special thank you to Michael H. Broder of the HIV Here & Now Project; he inspired me to write current poems, while showing the world that there is still a lot to say about HIV. Thank you to the readers who gave me feedback and supported me in being brave: Andrew Ramer, Jan Steckel, Risa Denenberg. And to the many legions of writers through time who have supported my writing. Thank you to Storme Webber who worked with me on an early draft when she was the Hugo House Writer in Residence. Thank you to the love of my life, John Perkins, who gave me the go-ahead and deep structural support to come out to the world. He also took the photo that is on the back cover and he is the staff of my existence. I am ever grateful to have such deep connection to such a strong partner in this lifetime.

This book is dedicated to the Babes Network, who helped me through the early difficult years. We have shown the world it is possible to thrive despite one of the biggest health epidemics. We are survivors, including those who passed, and it is courage that carries us forward. My love to the many Babes, past and present: Jesse, Pat, Barbara, Dori, Sue, Kass, Ally, Whitney, Dawn, Kelly, and so many more.

BIOGRAPHY

Julene Tripp Weaver is a Native New Yorker who moved to the northwest in 1989. She is currently a writer and psychotherapist in Seattle, Washington. Her two poetry books include her chapbook, *Case Walking: An AIDS Case Manager Wails Her Blues* (*Finishing Line Press*, 2007) and *No Father Can Save Her* (*Plainview Press*, 2011), which has autobiographical poetry about family and women's sexuality based on her experience growing up during the sexual revolution in New York City. Her undergraduate degree is in Creative Writing, her master's degree in Counseling.

David Whyte's book, *Consolations: The Solace, Nourishment and Underlying Meaning of Everyday Words,* helped Julene create an entry point to access her own vulnerability. In addressing vulnerability in his book David writes, "The only choice we have as we mature is how we inhabit our vulnerability, how we become larger and more courageous and more compassionate through our intimacy with disappearance, our choice is to inhabit vulnerability as generous citizens of loss, robustly and fully, or conversely, as misers and complainers, reluctant and fearful, always at the gates of existence, but never bravely and completely attempting to enter, never wanting to risk ourselves, never walking fully through the door."

Julene Tripp Weaver worked over twenty years as an AIDS case manager, an Adherence Counselor, and in AIDS education. In addition, she is a founder of the Babes Network. Supporting their early move to become a nonprofit, she led the committee that came up with the slogan, "A Sisterhood of Women Facing HIV Together," and served as their second Board President. She started the Health Corner Column in their newsletter where she wrote articles about health and healing using an herbal complementary approach, another one of her interests that she has studied widely.

In addition to poetry, Julene is writing a memoir and one of her creative nonfiction pieces is published *In The Words of Women International 2016 Anthology* by Yellow Chair Press. She studied fiction writing with Tom

Spanbauer, who trademarked "Dangerous Writing."

Julene Tripp Weaver's poetry is widely published in many print and online journals, including *Anti-Heroin Chic, Riverbabble, River & South Review, Cliterature, Menacing Hedge, Red Headed Stepchild Magazine, Snow Monkey, Nerve Cowboy, The Far Field, The Seattle Review of Books, The Unprecedented Review,* and *HIV Here & Now.* Julene's poetry has also been chosen for many anthologies including: *Spaces Between Us: Poetry, Prose and Art on HIV/AIDS, The Poeming Pigeon Poems on Music,* and in *Ice Cream,* and *Bang!*

Follow her on Twitter @trippweavepoet, on SoundCloud, and check out her website: www.julenetrippweaver.com.

CPSIA information can be obtained
at www.ICGtesting.com
Printed in the USA
FFOW03n0128280317
33860FF